Ancestors of Mark Edward Simmons

Generation 1

1. **Mark Edward Simmons**, son of Edward Wilton Simmons and Leona Ryals was born on 29 Oct 1967. He married **Diana Gail Edwards** on 23 Dec 1988 in Plant City, Florida. She was born on 28 Mar 1969 in Plant City, Florida. He married **Sherri (unknown)**. He married **Nancy Santiago Claridy**.

Generation 2

2. **Edward Wilton Simmons**, son of Edward Simmons and Monteen Turner was born on 29 Aug 1935 in Georgia. He died on 23 Apr 1997 in Hillsborough County, Florida. He married **Leona Ryals**.

3. **Leona Ryals**, daughter of Grimshaw Ryals and Tullue Deal was born on 14 Aug 1939 in Georgia.

More About Edward Wilton Simmons:
Burial: Hopewell Memorial Gardens, Plant City, Florida

Leona Ryals and Edward Wilton Simmons had the following child:

1.   i. Mark Edward Simmons, son of Edward Wilton Simmons and Leona Ryals was born on 29 Oct 1967. He married Diana Gail Edwards on 23 Dec 1988 in Plant City, Florida. She was born on 28 Mar 1969 in Plant City, Florida. He married Sherri (unknown). He married Nancy Santiago Claridy.

Generation 3

4. **Edward Simmons**, son of Benjamin Franklin Simmons and Nancy Ann Johnson was born about 1912 in Georgia. He married **Monteen Turner**.

5. **Monteen Turner**, daughter of Albert Oliver Turner and Lousiana Canup was born on 28 Feb 1916 in Hall County, Georgia. She died on 16 Jun 1984 in Brunswick, Georgia.

More About Edward Simmons:
Living In: 1920 Surrency, Georgia
Living In: 1930 Deems, Georgia

I0775955

More About Monteen Turner:
Burial: 19 Jun 1984 in Pleasant Grove Cemetery, Baxley, Georgia
Living In: 1984 Sterling Community, Glynn County, Georgia
Occupation: Worked thirty years for SeaPak Shrimp Company on St. Simons Island, Glynn County, Georgia

Notes for Monteen Turner:

SIMMONS, Monteen (Turner)
The Brunswick News; Monday 18 June 1984; pg. 3A col. 5

SIMMONS FUNERAL BEING HELD TODAY
Services for Monteen Turner Simmons, 68, a resident of Sterling who died early Saturday at the Glynn-Brunswick Memorial Hospital after a short illness will be held Tuesday.
She was a native of Appling County and had been a resident of Glynn County for the past 35 years. She had been employed by Sea-Pak for the past 30 years. She was a member of the Holiness Church in Baxley.
She is survived by two daughters, Willene Lott of St. Simons and Lulene Tison of Sterling. Two sons, Edward W. Simmons of Plant City, Fla. and Gary Simmons of Sterling; two sisters, Irene Carter of Baxley and Pauline Sellers of Savannah; a brother Bill Turner of Baxley; seven

grandchildren; two great-grandchildren; several nieces and nephews.
Services will be held Tuesday at 1 p.m. in the chapel of Edo Miller & Sons Funeral with the Rev. Dorris Black officiating. Entombment services will be held at 3:30 p.m. in Pleasant Grove Cemetery near Baxley.
The family will receive friends at the funeral home tonight from 6 until 9
o'clock. Edo Miller & Sons Funeral Home is in charge of arrangements.

Monteen Turner and Edward Simmons had the following children:

2.   i. Edward Wilton Simmons, son of Edward Simmons and Monteen Turner was born on 29 Aug 1935 in Georgia. He died on 23 Apr 1997 in Hillsborough County, Florida. He married Leona Ryals. She was born on 14 Aug 1939 in Georgia.

    ii. Willeen Simmons. She married Archie Lott.

    iii. Lulleen Simmons. She married Butch Tison.

    iv. Gary Simmons, son of Edward Simmons and Monteen Turner was born in Glynn County, Georgia.

    v. Infant Daughter Simmons, daughter of Edward Simmons and Monteen Turner was born on 14 Jul 1956 in Glynn County, Georgia. She died on 14 Jul 1956.

6. **Grimshaw Ryals**, son of Smith Ryals and Annie Laura Howard was born on 25 May 1913 in Liberty County, Georgia. He died on 13 Aug 1990 in Richmond County, Georgia. He married **Tullue Deal**.

7. **Tullue Deal**, daughter of James Walter Deal and Eva E. Rowe was born on 15 Aug 1912 in Georgia. She died on 02 Mar 2006 in Florida.

More About Grimshaw Ryals:
Burial: Hardshell Baptist Church Cemetery, Darien, McIntosh County, Georgia
Living In: 1920 Barrington, Georgia
Living In: 1990 Blythe, Georgia
Occupation: Truck Driver
Military Service: 14 Dec 1944; Enlisted in U.S. Army at Fort McPherson, Georgia.

More About Tullue Deal:
Burial: Hopewell Memorial Gardens, Plant City, Hillsborough County, Florida

Notes for Tullue Deal:
Social Security death index gives a birth date of August 15, 1911.
Buried next to her son, Grimshaw.

Tullue Deal and Grimshaw Ryals had the following children:

    i. Kenneth Ryals, son of Grimshaw Ryals and Tullue Deal was born on 13 Apr 1937 in Savannah. Georgia. He died on 09 Apr 2008 in Brunswick, Georgia. He married Barbara Lucille Mumford. She was born on 23 Oct 1942. She died on 01 Oct 1989 in Brunswick, Georgia. He married Margaret Highsmith.

More About Kenneth Ryals:
Burial: Brunswick Memorial Park Cemetery, Brunswick, Glynn County, Georgia
Occupation: Route salesman for Coca-Cola.
Occupation: Owned his own car detailing business

Notes for Kenneth
Ryals: Obituary
Kenneth (Kenny) G. Ryals, 70, a resident of Brunswick died Wednesday evening at his residence. Funeral Services will be 10:00 AM Saturday in the chapel of Brunswick Memorial Park Funeral Home with Rev. Wayne Manning officiating. Interment will follow in Brunswick Memorial Park Cemetery. Mr. Ryals was born in Savannah and a resident of Glynn County for 49 years and a prior resident of Cox. He had retired from Coca-Cola where he was a route salesman. He owned and operated a car detailing business. He was a wonderful husband, father and grand father, and a friend to all. He was an avid Ford owner and was a collector of Ford cars and Coca-Cola memorabilia. He is survived by his wife, Margaret Highsmith Ryals of Brunswick, two daughters, Kimberly (Kim) Waters (Todd) of Brunswick, Shirley Bedford (Mike) of Millington, TN, four step daughters, Vanessa Lee (Harry) of Hoboken, Christine Turner (Bobby) and Lynn Willis (Travis) both of Nahunta, Tina Temples (Terry) of Woodbine, one step son, Max T. Drury (Rachel) of Waverly, two sisters, Leona Simmons and Juanita Williams of Plant City, FL, two brothers, Hiram (Scooter) Ryals (Beverly) of Riverview, FL and Eugene Ryals of Plant City, FL., three grandchildren, thirteen step grandchildren, and four step great grandchildren and several nieces and nephews. He was preceded in death by his first wife, Lucille, his parents, Grimshaw and Tulla Ryals and a brother, Jimmy Ryals. Active pallbearers will be, T. J. Waters, Skippy Howard, Billy Copeland, Steve Pello, Pat Pello, Peter Santiago (Pineapple), Jay Honeycutt and Arthur Sharpe. Honorary pallbearers will be present and former employees of Brunswick Coca-Cola, Staff of third floor St. Vincent Hospital, Dr. Phillip B. Aquila and Staff, Dr. Ossi and First Coast Oncology Staff, Todd Waters, Max Drury, Dr. Robert Thompson and Staff, and Cal Thompson. Family will receive friends from 6:00-8:00 PM Friday, April 11, 2008 at Brunswick Memorial Park Funeral Home. The family request that memorial contributions be made to Hospice of the Golden Isles. Brunswick Memorial Park Funeral Home in charge of arrangements.

More About Barbara Lucille Mumford:
Burial: Brunswick Memorial Park Cemetery, Brunswick, Glynn County, Georgia

ii.   Grimshaw Ryals, son of Grimshaw Ryals and Tullue Deal was born on 24 Mar 1944 in Savannah, Georgia. He died on 07 Mar 2004 in Plant City, Florida.

More About Grimshaw Ryals:
Burial: 10 Mar 2004 in Hopewell Memorial Gardens, Plant City, Florida

Notes for Grimshaw Ryals:
Buried next to his mother.

iii. Eva Juanita Ryals, daughter of Grimshaw Ryals and Tullue Deal was born on 09 Dec 1948 in Georgia. She died on 26 Jun 2010 in Plant City, Florida. She married John Lloyd Williams about 1978.

More About Eva Juanita Ryals:
Burial: 30 Jun 2010 in Hopewell Memorial Gardens, Plant City, Florida

Notes for Eva Juanita Ryals:
Juanita "Tiny" WILLIAMS
WILLIAMS, Juanita "Tiny," 61, of Plant City, Fla., departed this life June 26, 2010. She was
preceded in death by her brothers, Kenneth Ryals and Jimmy Ryals. She is survived by her husband of 32 years, John Lloyd Williams; daughter, Eva Driggs (David); grand-daughter, Amber Owens; siblings, Leona Simmons, Scooter Ryals (Bev), and Eugene Ryals; and many loving family members and friends. A celebration of life will take place at noon Wednesday, June 30, at Hopewell Funeral Home, 6005 State Road 39 S., Plant City, where the family will receive friends at 11 a.m. Interment will follow at Hopewell Memorial Gardens, Plant City. Expressions of condolence may be sent at www.hopewellfuneral.com

iv. Hiram Ryals.

3. v. Leona Ryals, daughter of Grimshaw Ryals and Tullue Deal was born on 14 Aug 1939 in Georgia. She married Edward Wilton Simmons. He was born on 29 Aug 1935 in Georgia. He died on 23 Apr 1997 in Hillsborough County, Florida. She married James Willie Wells on 24 Apr 2011 in Plant City, Florida. He was born on 10 Aug 1936 in South Carolina. She married Albert J. Davis.

vi. Eugene Ryals, son of Grimshaw Ryals and Tullue Deal was born in 1950. He married Carol Hester Yarbrough. She was born in 1952.

Generation 4

8. **Benjamin Franklin Simmons** was born in Jan 1872 in Georgia. He died between 08 Jan 1920-14 Apr 1930. He married **Nancy Ann Johnson**, daughter of Thomas H. Johnson and Courtney Jones about 1897.

9. **Nancy Ann Johnson**, daughter of Thomas H. Johnson and Courtney Jones was born on 11 Feb 1873 in Dooley County, Georgia. She died on 13 Feb 1966 in Appling County, Georgia.

More About Benjamin Franklin Simmons:
Living In: 1900 Rabbitville, Clinch County, Georgia
Living In: 1910 Graham, Appling County, Georgia
Living In: 1920 Surrency, Appling County, Georgia
Occupation: Farmer

More About Nancy Ann Johnson:
Burial: Ten Mile Creek Baptist Church Cemetery, Appling County, Georgia
Living In: 1930 As a widow in Deems, Appling County, Georgia

Notes for Nancy Ann Johnson:

Birth and death dates are from Ten Mile Creek Baptist Church Cemetery. Georgia death index gives birth year as 1873 and date of death as February 13, 1966.

Nancy Ann Johnson and Benjamin Franklin Simmons had the following children:

 i. Maude Bethel Simmons, daughter of Benjamin Franklin Simmons and Nancy Ann Johnson was born on 22 Feb 1899 in Georgia. She married Forest S. Sapp on 30 May 1929 in Appling County, Georgia. He was born about 1909 in Georgia.

 ii. Harvey Wesley Simmons, son of Benjamin Franklin Simmons and Nancy Ann Johnson was born on 22 Sep 1902 in Georgia.

 iii. Bertie Evelyn Simmons, daughter of Benjamin Franklin Simmons and Nancy Ann Johnson was born on 27 Sep 1904 in Appling County, Georgia. She died on 20 Nov 1934 in Deens, Appling County, Georgia. She married John James Crews on 22 Mar 1926 in Appling County, Georgia. He was born on 26 Sep 1906 in Baker County, Florida. He died on 14 Dec 1963 in Charlton County, Georgia.

 iv. Beulah Victoria Simmons, daughter of Benjamin Franklin Simmons and Nancy Ann Johnson was born on 15 Jan 1906 in Georgia. She died on 26 Nov 1973 in Georgia. She married C. M. Turner on 19 Aug 1933 in Appling County, Georgia.

More About Beulah Victoria Simmons:
Burial: Ten Mile Creek Baptist Church Cemetery, Appling County, Georgia

 v. Jessie Gertrude Simmons, daughter of Benjamin Franklin Simmons and Nancy Ann Johnson was born on 27 Jan 1907 in Baxley, Appling County, Georgia. She died on 20 Oct 1970 in Brunswick, Georgia. She married Robert Turner.

 vi. Rilla Rosseter Simmons, daughter of Benjamin Franklin Simmons and Nancy Ann Johnson was born on 12 Sep 1909 in Appling County, Georgia. She died on 13 Jan 1988 in Brunswick, Georgia. She married John Lewis Godley on 03 Jul 1938 in Camden, Georgia. He was born on 05 Dec 1907 in Camden, Georgia. He died on 17 May 2003 in Brunswick, Georgia.

More About Rilla Rosseter Simmons:
Burial: Palmetto Cemetery, Brunswick, Georgia

More About John Lewis Godley:
Burial: Palmetto Cemetery, Brunswick, Georgia

 vii. Frances Mae Simmons, daughter of Benjamin Franklin Simmons and Nancy Ann Johnson was born about 1911 in Georgia.

4. viii. Edward Simmons, son of Benjamin Franklin Simmons and Nancy Ann Johnson was born about 1912 in Georgia. He married Monteen Turner. She was born on 28 Feb 1916 in Hall County, Georgia. She died on 16 Jun 1984 in Brunswick, Georgia.

 ix. Willis C. Simmons, son of Benjamin Franklin Simmons and Nancy Ann Johnson was born about 1915 in Georgia.

 x. Benjamin F. Simmons, son of Benjamin Franklin Simmons and Nancy Ann Johnson was born about Jun 1916 in Georgia. He died in 1934.

xi. Elizabeth V. Simmons, daughter of Benjamin Franklin Simmons and Nancy Ann Johnson was born about Apr 1919 in Georgia.

10. **Albert Oliver Turner**, son of William Franklin Turner and Vada Payne was born on 03 Feb 1897 in Hall County, Georgia. He died on 29 Sep 1976 in Chatham County, Georgia. He married **Lousiana Canup**, daughter of Newton James Canup and Nancy Amanda Jenkins in Hall County, Georgia.

11. **Lousiana Canup**, daughter of Newton James Canup and Nancy Amanda Jenkins was born on 19 Aug 1896 in Hall County, Georgia. She died on 25 Apr 1965 in Baxley, Georgia.

More About Albert Oliver Turner:
Burial: Old Pleasant Grove Cemetery, Appling County, Georgia
Living In: 1900 Polksville District, Hall County, Georgia
Living In: 1920 Narramore District, Hall County, Georgia
Living In: 1930 Appling County, Georgia
Living In 1976   Baxley, Georgia
Occupation: Farmer

Notes for Albert Oliver Turner:
World War One draft registration gives birth date as February 3, 1897. Headstone gives birth date as January 3, 1899. Birth date in 1900 Federal census is January 1897. Social security death index gives birthdate as January 3, 1899.

More About Lousiana Canup:
Burial: 27 Apr 1965 in Old Pleasant Grove Cemetery, Appling County, Georgia
Occupation: 1920; Works on horse farm

Notes for Lousiana Canup:
Used Lucy instead of Lousiana for given name.
Family members remember her maiden name as Canup. Funeral home records show her parents as Amanda Jenkins and Tom Bryant.

Lousiana Canup and Albert Oliver Turner had the following children:

5. i. Monteen Turner, daughter of Albert Oliver Turner and Lousiana Canup was born on 28 Feb 1916 in Hall County, Georgia. She died on 16 Jun 1984 in Brunswick, Georgia. She married Edward Simmons. He was born about 1912 in Georgia.

iii. Talmadge Turner, son of Albert Oliver Turner and Lousiana Canup was born on 27 Sep 1917 in Hall County, Georgia. He died on 16 Aug 1983 in Baxley, Georgia. He married Inez Altman on 08 Jan 1945 in Appling County, Georgia. She was born on 2 Oct 1928 in Georgia. She died on 01 Jul 2007 in Baxley, Georgia.

    More About Talmadge Turner:
    Burial: Old Pleasant Grove Cemetery, Appling County, Georgia

    More About Inez Altman:
    Burial: Old Pleasant Grove Cemetery, Appling County, Georgia

iii. Irene Turner, daughter of Albert Oliver Turner and Lousiana Canup was born on 30 Jun 1922 in Hall County, Georgia. She died on 07 Aug 1988 in Appling County,

Georgia. She married James B. Carter, son of James Carter and Allie Sapp on 06 Jun 1942 in Appling County, Georgia. He was born on 29 Mar 1924 in Appling County, Georgia. He died on 29 Jul 2003 in Appling County, Georgia.

More About Irene Turner:
Burial: Appling County, Georgia

More About James B. Carter:
Burial: 31 Jul 2003 in Appling County, Georgia
Occupation: Sheriff of Appling County, Georgia August 1960-1976
Occupation: Chief of Police, Baxley, Georgia, 1976-1979
Military Service: U.S. Army, World War Two

  iv. William Thomas Turner, son of Albert Oliver Turner and Lousiana Canup was born on 10 Nov 1925 in Hall County, Georgia. He died on 05 Aug 2004 in Appling County, Georgia. He married Eleanor Lightsey, daughter of Kenneth Lightsey and Myrtle Tyre in Appling County, Georgia. She was born on 06 Jul 1931 in Appling County, Georgia. She died on 18 Feb 1994 in Appling County, Georgia.

   More About William Thomas Turner:
   Burial: 06 Aug 2004 in Pine Grove Freewill Baptist Church, Appling County, Georgia

   More About Eleanor Lightsey:
   Burial: Pine Grove Freewill Baptist Church, Appling County, Georgia

  v. Pauline Turner, daughter of Albert Oliver Turner and Lousiana Canup was born on 10 Nov 1928 in Appling County, Georgia. She died on 29 Oct 2002 in Appling County, Georgia. She married Dwight Sellers. He was born in Appling County, Georgia.

   More About Pauline Turner:
   Burial: 01 Nov 2002 in Zion Baptist Church Cemetery, Appling County, Georgia

  vi. infant daughter Turner.

12. **Smith Ryals**, son of Jabez D. Ryals and Sarah Amos was born on 23 Dec 1871 in Georgia. He died on 15 Apr 1946 in McIntosh County, Georgia. He married **Annie Laura Howard**, daughter of (unknown) Howard and (unknown) in 1894.

13. **Annie Laura Howard**, daughter of (unknown) Howard and (unknown) was born on 23 Dec 1874 in Georgia. She died on 05 Jan 1942 in Georgia.

More About Smith Ryals:
Burial: Hardshell Baptist Church Cemetery, Darien, McIntosh County, Georgia
Living In: 1880 Darien, Georgia
Living In: 1900 Barrington, McIntosh County, Georgia
Living In: 1910 McIntosh County, Georgia
Living In: 1920 Barrington, McIntosh County, Georgia

Living In: 1930 Jones, McIntosh County, Georgia
Occupation: 1900; Farmer

More About Annie Laura Howard:
Burial: Hardshell Baptist Church Cemetery, Darien, McIntosh County, Georgia

Annie Laura Howard and Smith Ryals had the following children:

    i.   Reuben L. Ryals, son of Smith Ryals and Annie Laura Howard was born on 10 Oct 1895 in Georgia. He died on 04 Nov 1967 in Georgia.

    ii.

       More About Reuben L. Ryals:
       Burial: Hardshell Baptist Church Cemetery, Darien, McIntosh County, Georgia

    iii.   Ephraim Ryals, son of Smith Ryals and Annie Laura Howard was born on 30 Jan 1896 in Georgia. He died on 31 Jan 1966 in Georgia.

       More About Ephraim Ryals:
       Burial: Hardshell Baptist Church Cemetery, Darien, McIntosh County, Georgia Military Service: Quartermaster Corps, World War One

    iv.   Betty Ryals, daughter of Smith Ryals and Annie Laura Howard was born in Feb 1899 in Georgia.

    v.   Luther Ryals, son of Smith Ryals and Annie Laura Howard was born about 1901 in Georgia.

    vi.   Jeslo Ryals, son of Smith Ryals and Annie Laura Howard was born on 11 Feb 1905 in Georgia. He died in May 1960 in Georgia.

       More About Jeslo Ryals:
       Burial: Hardshell Baptist Church Cemetery, Darien, McIntosh County, Georgia

    vii.   Freddy Ryals, son of Smith Ryals and Annie Laura Howard was born about 1907 in Georgia.

    viii.   Bertha Ryals, daughter of Smith Ryals and Annie Laura Howard was born about Dec 1909 in Georgia.

6.   viii. Grimshaw Ryals, son of Smith Ryals and Annie Laura Howard was born on 25 May 1913 in Liberty County, Georgia. He died on 13 Aug 1990 in Richmond County, Georgia. He married Tullue Deal. She was born on 15 Aug 1912 in Georgia. She died on 02 Mar 2006 in Florida.

    ix.   Morris Ryals, son of Smith Ryals and Annie Laura Howard was born about 1914 in Georgia.

14.   **James Walter Deal**, son of John Washington Deal and Susan Ann Rowe was born in Jan 1878 in Georgia. He died on 09 Apr 1960 in McIntosh County, Georgia. He married **Eva E. Rowe**, daughter of Jones Allen Rowe and Mary E. Morgan on 27 Jun 1910 in McIntosh County, Georgia.

15.   **Eva E. Rowe**, daughter of Jones Allen Rowe and Mary E. Morgan was born on 14 Apr 1874 in Georgia. She died on 21 Apr 1928 in McIntosh County, Georgia.

More About James Walter Deal:
Living In: 1930 McIntosh County, Georgia
Occupation: 1920; Farmer, McIntosh County, Georgia

More About Eva E. Rowe:
Burial: 22 Apr 1928
Living In: 1910 McIntosh County, Georgia

Notes for Eva E. Rowe:
Walter Deal was listed in 1910 census as a brother in law to Eva and in the 1920 census
as spouse and head of household.

Eva E. Rowe and James Walter Deal had the following children:
7.   i. Tullue Deal, daughter of James Walter Deal and Eva E. Rowe was born on 15 Aug 1912
               in Georgia. She died on 02 Mar 2006 in Florida. She married Grimshaw Ryals. He was
               born on 25 May 1913 in Liberty County, Georgia. He died on 13 Aug 1990 in
               Richmond County, Georgia.
           ii. Elija Deal, son of James Walter Deal and Eva E. Rowe was born about 1917
               in Georgia.

Generation 5

18.   **Thomas H. Johnson** was born about 1834 in North Carolina. He died about 1879 in Appling County,
       Georgia. He married **Courtney Jones**, daughter of Theophilus Jones and Zylphia Hutto on
       29 Mar 1866 in Dooly County, Georgia.

19.   **Courtney Jones**, daughter of Theophilus Jones and Zylphia Hutto was born on 22 Apr 1839
       in Dooley County, Georgia. She died on 08 Feb 1932 in Appling County, Georgia.

       More About Thomas H. Johnson:
       Living In: 1870 Mitchell County, Georgia
       Occupation: 1870 - Farm Labor

       Notes for Thomas H. Johnson:
       Birth year is from 1870 U.S. census.

       More About Courtney Jones:
       Burial: Bethel Free Will Baptist Church Cemetery, Appling County,
       Georgia
       Living In: 1860 With her parents in Dooly County, Georgia
       Living In: 1880 As a widow in Dooly County, Georgia

       Notes for Courtney Jones:
       1860 and 1870 U. S. census reports indicate a birth date of about 1847. 1880 U.S. census gives
       a birth year of 1843.

       Courtney Jones and Thomas H. Johnson had the following children:
            i.   James Henry Johnson, son of Thomas H. Johnson and Courtney Jones was
                   born on 08 Nov 1867 in Georgia. He died on 20 Aug 1930 in Kirkland, Georgia.
                   He married Sarah E. (unknown). She was born in 1875. She died in 1955.

                   More About James Henry Johnson:

Burial: 21 Aug 1930 in Antioch Baptist Church Cemetery, Kirkland,
Georgia
Occupation: Farmer

More About Sarah E. (unknown):
Burial: Antioch Baptist Church Cemetery, Kirkland, Georgia

  ii. Thomas Johnson, son of Thomas H. Johnson and Courtney Jones was born
about 1872 in Georgia.

9. iii. Nancy Ann Johnson, daughter of Thomas H. Johnson and Courtney Jones was born on
11 Feb 1873 in Dooley County, Georgia. She died on 13 Feb 1966 in Appling County,
Georgia. She married Benjamin Franklin Simmons about 1897. He was born in Jan
1872 in Georgia. He died between 08 Jan 1920-14 Apr 1930.

  iv. Zylphia Henrietta Johnson, daughter of Thomas H. Johnson and Courtney Jones
was born on 01 Jan 1874 in Georgia. She died on 30 Nov 1941 in Ware County,
Georgia. She married James Elizah Jones. He was born on 21 Jan 1874 in
Appling County, Georgia. He died on 12 Jul 1937 in Ware County, Georgia.

More About Zylphia Henrietta Johnson:
Burial: Friendship Freewill Baptist Church Cemetery, Millwood, Ware
County, Georgia

More About James Elizah Jones:
Burial: Friendship Freewill Baptist Church Cemetery, Millwood, Ware
County, Georgia
Military Service: Company L, 3rd U.S. Volunteer Infantry, Spanish American War

  v. Leola Johnson, daughter of Thomas H. Johnson and Courtney Jones was born
on 22 Apr 1878 in Georgia. She died on 15 Sep 1970 in Brunswick. Georgia.

  vi. Joseph Johnson, son of Thomas H. Johnson and Courtney Jones was born on
25 Jun 1879 in Georgia. He died on 11 Sep 1952 in Georgia. He married Ruth
Elizabeth Harden. She was born on 09 Feb 1888 in Georgia. She died on 06
Mar 1926 in Appling County, Georgia.

More About Joseph Johnson:
Burial: Bethel Freewill Baptist Church Cemetery, Appling County,
Georgia
Living In: 1910 Graham, Appling County, Georgia
Living In: 1920 Graham, Appling County, Georgia
Occupation: Farmer

Notes for Joseph Johnson:
Joseph is not with his mother, Courtney, on the 1880 U.S. census. A number of his
relatives believe he is a son of Thomas H. Johnson and Courtney Jones. 1910 U.S.
census gives a birth year of Abt.1882. 1920 U.S. census gives a birth year of Abt.
1881. Having a daughter named Zylphia could indicate a connection with
Courtney Jones, who had a daughter named Zylphia and Courtney's mother, who
was named Zylphia.

More About Ruth Elizabeth Harden:
Burial: Bethel Freewill Baptist Church Cemetery, Appling County, Georgia

Notes for Ruth Elizabeth Harden:
Death certificate has February 9, 1888 as date of birth. Cemetery has February 15, 1888 as date of birth.

20. **William Franklin Turner**, son of James Jarrett Turner and Mary Elizabeth Dyer was born on 03 Jul 1861 in Union County, Georgia. He died on 20 Aug 1919 in Banks County, Georgia. He married **Vada Payne**.

21. **Vada Payne** was born in Mar 1869 in Georgia.

More About William Franklin Turner:
Living In: 1900 Polksville District, Hall County, Georgia
Occupation: Farmer

Vada Payne and William Franklin Turner had the following children:

    i.   Etta Mae Turner, daughter of William Franklin Turner and Vada Payne was born in Dec 1884 in Georgia.

    ii.   James Andrew Turner, son of William Franklin Turner and Vada Payne was born in Jun 1887 in Georgia. He died on 09 Mar 1948 in Baldwin County, Georgia. He married Viola Jesse Buffington. She was born on 31 Aug 1886 in Hall County, Georgia. She died on 26 Jul 1978 in Hall County, Georgia.

        More About James Andrew Turner:
        Living In: 1948 Hall County, Georgia
        Occupation: 1900; Farm Labor

    iii.   Joseph Turner, son of William Franklin Turner and Vada Payne was born in Apr 1889 in Georgia.

        More About Joseph Turner:
        Occupation: 1900; Farm Labor

    iv.   Claude Livingston Turner, son of William Franklin Turner and Vada Payne was born on 05 Jun 1891 in Georgia. He died on 30 Sep 1962 in Baldwin County, Georgia. He married Rader Dodd. She was born on 07 Nov 1897. She died on 26 Jan 1964 in Hall County, Georgia.

        More About Claude Livingston Turner:
        Burial: Bellton Baptist Church Cemetery, Hall County, Georgia
        Living In: Sep 1962 Hall County, Georgia

        More About Rader Dodd:
        Burial: Bellton Baptist Church Cemetery, Hall County, Georgia

v.   Walter Turner, son of William Franklin Turner and Vada Payne was born in Apr 1894 in Georgia.

10.   vi. Albert Oliver Turner, son of William Franklin Turner and Vada Payne was born on 03 Feb 1897 in Hall County, Georgia. He died on 29 Sep 1976 in Chatham County, Georgia. He married Lousiana Canup, daughter of Newton James Canup and Nancy Amanda Jenkins in Hall County, Georgia. She was born on 19 Aug 1896 in Hall County, Georgia. She died on 25 Apr 1965 in Baxley, Georgia.

vii.   Sallie Turner, daughter of William Franklin Turner and Vada Payne was born in Sep 1899 in Georgia.

22.   **Newton James Canup**, son of Jacob Canup and Mary Ann Crow was born on 03 Jun 1864 in Habersham County, Georgia. He died on 31 Aug 1936 in Appling County, Georgia. He married **Nancy Amanda Jenkins**, daughter of John Jenkins and Elizabeth (unknown) on 11 Mar 1889 in Hall County, Georgia.

23.   **Nancy Amanda Jenkins**, daughter of John Jenkins and Elizabeth (unknown) was born in May 1875 in Hall County, Georgia. She died in Appling County, Georgia.

More About Newton James Canup:
Living In: 1900 Narramore District, Hall County, Georgia
Living In: 1920 Nanramore District, Hall County, Georgia
Living In: 1930 Appling County, Georgia
Occupation: Farmer

More About Nancy Amanda Jenkins:
b: May 1875

Nancy Amanda Jenkins and Newton James Canup had the following children:
i.   Cora Lee Canup, daughter of Newton James Canup and Nancy Amanda Jenkins was born on 24 Dec 1890 in Hall County, Georgia. She died on 22 Aug 1980 in Baxley, Georgia. She married William Franklin Turner. He was born on 03 Jul 1861 in Union County, Georgia. He died on 20 Aug 1919 in Banks County, Georgia. She married David Chapman Carter. He was born on 10 Aug 1890. He died on 30 Dec 1966 in Jeff Davis County, Georgia.

More About Cora Lee Canup:
Burial: 24 Aug 1980 in Ten Mile Creek Baptist Church Cemetery, Baxley, Appling County, Georgia
Living In: 1920 Cora and her children are living with her parents in Narramore District, Hall County, Georgia

More About William Franklin Turner:
Living In: 1900 Polksville District, Hall County, Georgia
Occupation: Farmer

More About David Chapman Carter:
Burial: Ten Mile Creek Baptist Church Cemetery, Baxley, Appling County, Georgia
Living In: 1966 Appling County, Georgia

ii.   Nora Canup, daughter of Newton James Canup and Nancy Amanda Jenkins
       was born on 26 Dec 1894 in Georgia. She died on 27 Mar 1962 in Wayne
       County, Georgia. She married John Henry Jenkins. He was born on 15 Jul 1874
       in Hall County, Georgia. He died on 02 Jun 1959 in Appling County, Georgia.

       More About Nora Canup:
       Burial: Pleasant Grove Cemetery, Appling County,
       Georgia
       Living In: 1962 Appling County, Georgia

       More About John Henry Jenkins:
       Living In: 1930 Deens, Appling County, Georgia

11.   iii. Lousiana Canup, daughter of Newton James Canup and Nancy Amanda Jenkins was
       born on 19 Aug 1896 in Hall County, Georgia. She died on 25 Apr 1965 in Baxley,
       Georgia. She married Albert Oliver Turner, son of William Franklin Turner and Vada
       Payne in Hall County, Georgia. He was born on 03 Feb 1897 in Hall County,
       Georgia. He died on 29 Sep 1976 in Chatham County, Georgia.

24.   **Jabez D. Ryals** was born about 1826 in Georgia. He died on 01 Aug 1904 in Georgia. He married
       Sarah Amos.

25.   **Sarah Amos**, daughter of Jonathan Amos and Mary Ann Rozier was born about 1835 in
       Georgia. She died on 16 May 1906 in Georgia.

       More About Jabez D. Ryals:
       Burial: Plum Orchard Cemetery, Cox, McIntosh County,
       Georgia Living In: 1850 in McIntosh County, Georgia
       Living In: 1860 McIntosh County, Georgia
       Living In: 1870 McIntosh County, Georgia
       Living In: 1880 Darien, McIntosh County, Georgia
       Living In: 1900 Barrington, McIntosh County, Georgia
       Military Service: May 21, 1862 - May 17, 1864, Company K, 5th Georgia Cavalry, C.S.A.

       Notes for Jabez D. Ryals:
       Jabez was 36 years old on May 21, 1862 when he was mustered in with the First Battalion
       of Georgia Cavalry which was later part of the 5th Regiment of Georgia Cavalry.

       More About Sarah Amos:
       Burial: Plum Orchard Cemetery, Cox, McIntosh County, Georgia

       Sarah Amos and Jabez D. Ryals had the following children:
       i.   Ruth Ryals, daughter of Jabez D. Ryals and Sarah Amos was born about 1849
              in Georgia.

       ii.   Catherine Ryals, daughter of Jabez D. Ryals and Sarah Amos was born about
              1852 in Georgia.

       iii.   Madison Ryals, son of Jabez D. Ryals and Sarah Amos was born about 1855
              in Georgia.

       iv.   Lavinia Ryals, daughter of Jabez D. Ryals and Sarah Amos was born about 1857 in

Georgia.

v.   Beauregard Ryals, son of Jabez D. Ryals and Sarah Amos was born in 1861 in Georgia. He died in 1934 in Georgia. He married Nettie J. (unknown). She was born in 1870. She died in 1935.

More About Beauregard Ryals:
Burial: Hardshell Baptist Church Cemetery, Darien, McIntosh County, Georgia Living In: 1900 in Barrington, McIntosh County, Georgia

More About Nettie J. (unknown):
Burial: Hardshell Baptist Church Cemetery, Darien, McIntosh County, Georgia

vi.   Mary Ryals, daughter of Jabez D. Ryals and Sarah Amos was born about 1862 in Georgia.

vii.   Israel Ryals, son of Jabez D. Ryals and Sarah Amos was born on 08 Mar 1866 in Georgia. He died on 03 Nov 1949 in Georgia. He married Minnie (unknown). She was born on 15 Oct 1872 in Georgia. She died on 16 Apr 1943 in Georgia.

More About Israel Ryals:
Burial: Hardshell Baptist Church Cemetery, Darien, McIntosh County, Georgia Living In: 1900 in Barrington, McIntosh County, Georgia

More About Minnie (unknown):
Burial: Hardshell Baptist Church Cemetery, Darien, McIntosh County, Georgia

viii.   Serapha Ryals, daughter of Jabez D. Ryals and Sarah Amos was born about 1870 in Georgia.

12.   ix. Smith Ryals, son of Jabez D. Ryals and Sarah Amos was born on 23 Dec 1871 in Georgia. He died on 15 Apr 1946 in McIntosh County, Georgia. He married Annie Laura Howard, daughter of (unknown) Howard and (unknown) in 1894. She was born on 23 Dec 1874 in Georgia. She died on 05 Jan 1942 in Georgia.

26.   **(unknown) Howard**. He married **(unknown)**.

27.   **(unknown)**.

More About (unknown):
Living In: 1880 Hall County, Georgia

(unknown) and (unknown) Howard had the following children:

i.   Stargel D. Howard, son of (unknown) Howard and (unknown) was born about 1871 in Georgia.

14.   ii. Annie Laura Howard, daughter of (unknown) Howard and (unknown) was born on 23 Dec 1874 in Georgia. She died on 05 Jan 1942 in Georgia. She married Smith Ryals, son of Jabez D. Ryals and Sarah Amos in 1894. He was born on 23 Dec

1871 in Georgia. He died on 15 Apr 1946 in McIntosh County, Georgia.

    iii.   Eddie T. Howard, son of (unknown) Howard and (unknown) was born about 1876 in Georgia.

28.   **John Washington Deal**, son of Curtis Deal and Frances Gill was born in Apr 1848. He died on 21 Nov 1926 in McIntosh County, Georgia. He married **Susan Ann Rowe** on 16 Jan 1868 in Liberty County, Georgia.

29.   **Susan Ann Rowe** was born in Aug 1843. She died before 21 Nov

1926. More About John Washington Deal:

Born April 1848 in Georgia
Living In: 1880 McIntosh County, Georgia
Living In: 1900 McIntosh County, Georgia
Occupation: Farmer

More About Susan Ann Rowe:
b: Aug 1843 in Georgia
Living In: 1910 McIntosh County, Georgia

Susan Ann Rowe and John Washington Deal had the following children:

    i.   Jones A. Deal, son of John Washington Deal and Susan Ann Rowe was born about 1868 in Georgia.

    ii.   Zachariah Deal, son of John Washington Deal and Susan Ann Rowe was born in Mar 1871 in Georgia. He married Eva E. Rowe, daughter of Jones Allen Rowe and Mary E. Morgan on 27 Sep 1896 in McIntosh County, Georgia. She was born on 14 Apr 1874 in Georgia. She died on 21 Apr 1928 in McIntosh County, Georgia.

        More   About   Zachariah
        Deal: Occupation: Farmer

        More About Eva E. Rowe:
        Burial: 22 Apr 1928
        Living In: 1910 McIntosh County, Georgia

        Notes for Eva E. Rowe:
        Walter Deal was listed in 1910 census as a brother in law to Eva and in the 1920 census as spouse and head of household.

    iii.   Alice Deal, daughter of John Washington Deal and Susan Ann Rowe was born about 1873 in Georgia.

    iv.   Mary J. Deal, daughter of John Washington Deal and Susan Ann Rowe was born about 1875 in Georgia.

    v.   Willie O. Deal, son of John Washington Deal and Susan Ann Rowe was born about 1877 in Georgia.

14.   vi.   James Walter Deal, son of John Washington Deal and Susan Ann Rowe was born

in Jan 1878 in Georgia. He died on 09 Apr 1960 in McIntosh County, Georgia. He married Eva E. Rowe, daughter of Jones Allen Rowe and Mary E. Morgan on 27 Jun 1910 in McIntosh County, Georgia. She was born on 14 Apr 1874 in Georgia. She died on 21 Apr 1928 in McIntosh County, Georgia.

    vii.   Elliot Deal, son of John Washington Deal and Susan Ann Rowe was born about 1880 in Georgia.

    viii.   John W. Deal, son of John Washington Deal and Susan Ann Rowe was born in Jun 1881 in Georgia.

    ix.   Francis Deal, son of John Washington Deal and Susan Ann Rowe was born in Jun 1884 in Georgia.

    x.   Rudolph Deal, son of John Washington Deal and Susan Ann Rowe was born in Feb 1886 in Georgia.

    xi.   Aggie F. Deal, daughter of John Washington Deal and Susan Ann Rowe was born in Apr 1888 in Georgia.

    xii.   Charley Deal, son of John Washington Deal and Susan Ann Rowe was born in May 1890 in Georgia.

30.   **Jones Allen Rowe** was born about 1815 in Georgia. He married **Mary E. Morgan** on 18 Dec 1873 in Liberty County, Georgia.

31.   **Mary E. Morgan** was born about 1834 in Georgia.

More About Jones Allen Rowe:
Living In: 1850 Liberty County, Georgia
Living In: 1880 Liberty County, Georgia
Occupation: Farmer

Mary E. Morgan and Jones Allen Rowe had the following children:

    i.   Samuel M. Rowe, son of Jones Allen Rowe and Mary E. Morgan was born about 1869 in Georgia.

    ii.   Ella M. Rowe, daughter of Jones Allen Rowe and Mary E. Morgan was born about 1872 in Georgia.

16.   iii. Eva E. Rowe, daughter of Jones Allen Rowe and Mary E. Morgan was born on 14 Apr 1874 in Georgia. She died on 21 Apr 1928 in McIntosh County, Georgia. She married James Walter Deal, son of John Washington Deal and Susan Ann Rowe on 27 Jun 1910 in McIntosh County, Georgia. He was born in Jan 1878 in Georgia. He died on 09 Apr 1960 in McIntosh County, Georgia. She married Zachariah Deal, son of John Washington Deal and Susan Ann Rowe on 27 Sep 1896 in McIntosh County, Georgia. He was born in Mar 1871 in Georgia.

Generation 6

38.   **Theophilus Jones** was born about 1805 in North Carolina. He married **Zylphia Hutto**.

39.   **Zylphia Hutto** was born about 1820 in Georgia.

More About Theophilus Jones:
Living In: 1860 Dooly County, Georgia

Zylphia Hutto and Theophilus Jones had the following children:

19.   i. Courtney Jones, daughter of Theophilus Jones and Zylphia Hutto was born on 22 Apr 1839 in Dooley County, Georgia. She died on 08 Feb 1932 in Appling County, Georgia. She married Thomas H. Johnson on 29 Mar 1866 in Dooly County, Georgia. He was born about 1834 in North Carolina. He died about 1879 in Appling County, Georgia.

     ii. Eliza Jones, daughter of Theophilus Jones and Zylphia Hutto was born about 1848 in Georgia.

     iii. Nancy Jones, daughter of Theophilus Jones and Zylphia Hutto was born about 1852 in Georgia.

     iv. Alice Jones, daughter of Theophilus Jones and Zylphia Hutto was born about 1854 in Georgia.

     v. John Jones, son of Theophilus Jones and Zylphia Hutto was born about 1856 in Georgia.

40. **James Jarrett Turner**, son of Jarrett Turner and Sarah Collins was born on 25 Jul 1840 in Habersham County, Georgia. He died on 30 Sep 1899 in Hall County, Georgia. He married **Mary Elizabeth Dyer**, daughter of Micajah Dyer and Harriet Hall on 28 Mar 1858 in Union County, Georgia.

41. **Mary Elizabeth Dyer**, daughter of Micajah Dyer and Harriet Hall was born in 1842 in Union County, Georgia. She died on 10 Nov 1910.

42.

More About James Jarrett Turner:
Living In: 1860 Union County, Georgia
Living In: 1870 Union County, Georgia
Living In: 1880 Naramore, Hall County, Georgia
Occupation: 1880; Running Grist Mill
Occupation: 1860 and 1870, Farmer

Mary Elizabeth Dyer and James Jarrett Turner had the following children:

     i. Micajah Lumpkin Turner, son of James Jarrett Turner and Mary Elizabeth Dyer was born on 26 Feb 1859 in Union County, Georgia.

21.   ii. William Franklin Turner, son of James Jarrett Turner and Mary Elizabeth Dyer was born on 03 Jul 1861 in Union County, Georgia. He died on 20 Aug 1919 in Banks County, Georgia. He married Vada Payne. She was born in Mar 1869 in Georgia. He married Cora Lee Canup. She was born on 24 Dec 1890 in Hall County, Georgia. She died on 22 Aug 1980 in Baxley, Georgia.

44. **Jacob Canup** was born about 1815 in North Carolina. He died in 1896. He married **Mary Ann Crow**.

45. **Mary Ann Crow**, daughter of James Crow was born about 1820 in Georgia. She died in 1911.

More About Jacob Canup:
Living In: 1850 District 4, Habersham County, Georgia
Living In: 1860 Habersham County, Georgia
Living In: 1870 Mud Creek District, Habersham County, Georgia
Living In: 1880 Narramore District, Hall County, Georgia
Occupation: 1870 - Farmer
Occupation: 1860 - Millwright and Farmer

Occupation: 1880 - Farmer
Occupation: 1850 - Millwright

Mary Ann Crow and Jacob Canup had the following children:

    i.   John Monroe Canup, son of Jacob Canup and Mary Ann Crow was born on 10 Jun 1841 in Habersham County, Georgia. He died on 17 Mar 1911 in Georgia. He married Mary Miranda Ferguson, daughter of Andrew Jackson Ferguson and Jane Higgins on 17 Jul 1866 in Habersham County, Georgia. She was born on 17 Mar 1846 in Georgia. She died on 17 Apr 1931 in Habersham County, Georgia.

    ii.   F. M. Canup, son of Jacob Canup and Mary Ann Crow was born about 1842 in Habersham County, Georgia.

    iii.   Margaret Caroline Canup, daughter of Jacob Canup and Mary Ann Crow was born about 1845 in Habersham County, Georgia. She died on 03 Jan 1914. She married William Jackson Ferguson. He was born on 17 Mar 1841 in Georgia. He died on 20 May 1924 in Towns County, Georgia.

    More About William Jackson Ferguson:
    Burial: 21 May 1924 in Burch Cemetery, Sunnyside, Towns County, Georgia

    iv.   Sarah Jane Canup, daughter of Jacob Canup and Mary Ann Crow was born about 1847 in Habersham County, Georgia.

    v.   William W. Canup, son of Jacob Canup and Mary Ann Crow was born in May 1848 in Habersham County, Georgia. He married Mary D. (unknown). She was born in Aug 1863 in Georgia.

    vi.   Miles D. Canup, son of Jacob Canup and Mary Ann Crow was born about 1851 in Habersham County, Georgia.

    vii.   Jacob C. Canup, son of Jacob Canup and Mary Ann Crow was born about 1854 in Habersham County, Georgia.

    viii.   Amanda M. Canup, daughter of Jacob Canup and Mary Ann Crow was born about 1857 in Habersham County, Georgia.

    ix.   Matthew H. Canup, son of Jacob Canup and Mary Ann Crow was born about 1858 in Habersham County, Georgia.

    x.   Cicero Canup, daughter of Jacob Canup and Mary Ann Crow was born about 1860 in Habersham County, Georgia.

22.   xi. Newton James Canup, son of Jacob Canup and Mary Ann Crow was born on 03 Jun 1864 in Habersham County, Georgia. He died on 31 Aug 1936 in Appling County, Georgia. He married Nancy Amanda Jenkins, daughter of John Jenkins and Elizabeth (unknown) on 11 Mar 1889 in Hall County, Georgia. She was born in May 1875 in Hall County, Georgia. She died in Appling County, Georgia.

46.   **John Jenkins** was born about 1817 in North Carolina. He married **Elizabeth (unknown)**.

47.   **Elizabeth (unknown)** was born in May 1845 in Georgia.

More About John Jenkins:
Living In: 1880 Glade District No. 403, Hall County, Georgia
Occupation: 1880; Running Corn Mill in Glade District No. 403, Hall County, Georgia

More About Elizabeth (unknown):
Living In: 1900 Glade District No. 403, Hall County, Georgia

Notes for Elizabeth (unknown):
Living next door to her son, John Henry, in 1900. Her daughter, Emma, is living with her.

Elizabeth (unknown) and John Jenkins had the following children:
   i.   Clifford Jenkins, daughter of John Jenkins and Elizabeth (unknown) was born about 1867 in Georgia.

   ii. Sarah Jenkins, daughter of John Jenkins and Elizabeth (unknown) was born on 16 Jun 1871 in Georgia. She died on 17 Nov 1932. She married W. A. J. Kidd. He was born on 02 Jan 1867. He died on 30 Jan 1948.

        More About Sarah Jenkins:
        Burial: Buffington Cemetery, Hall County, Georgia

        More About W. A. J. Kidd:
        Burial: Buffington Cemetery, Hall County, Georgia

   iii. Thomas Jenkins, son of John Jenkins and Elizabeth (unknown) was born about 1873 in Georgia. He died on 11 May 1936. He married Lula (unknown). She was born on 16 Oct 1875. She died on 27 Feb 1928.

        More About Thomas Jenkins:
        Burial: Bethlehem Baptist Church, Lula, Georgia

        More About Lula (unknown):
        Burial: Bethlehem Baptist Church, Lula, Georgia

23.   iv. Nancy Amanda Jenkins, daughter of John Jenkins and Elizabeth (unknown) was born in May 1875 in Hall County, Georgia. She died in Appling County, Georgia. She married Newton James Canup, son of Jacob Canup and Mary Ann Crow on 11 Mar 1889 in Hall County, Georgia. He was born on 03 Jun 1864 in Habersham County, Georgia. He died on 31 Aug 1936 in Appling County, Georgia.

        v.   Andrew H. Jenkins, son of John Jenkins and Elizabeth (unknown) was born about 1877 in Georgia.

        vi. Henry Jenkins, son of John Jenkins and Elizabeth (unknown) was born in Jul 1879 in Hall County, Georgia. He married Jessie Baugh on 02 Apr 1899 in Hall County, Georgia. She was born in Apr 1885 in Georgia.

        More About Henry Jenkins:

Living In: 1900 Glade District No. 403, Hall County, Georgia
Living In: 1910 Glade District No. 403, Hall County, Georgia

vii.   Emma Virginia Jenkins, daughter of John Jenkins and Elizabeth (unknown) was born in Jan 1887 in Lula, Georgia. She died on 21 Oct 1969. She married Steve Lewallen. He was born on 10 Jul 1886 in Birmingham, alabama. He died on 09 Feb 1954.

More About Emma Virginia Jenkins:
Burial: Bethlehem Baptist Church, Lula, Georgia

More About Steve Lewallen:
Burial: Bethlehem Baptist Church, Lula, Georgia

viii. Mary Jenkins, daughter of John Jenkins and Elizabeth (unknown) was born in Georgia. She married John Baugh. She married (unknown) Jones.

More About Mary Jenkins:
Burial: White Hill Baptist Church, Lula, Georgia

More About (unknown) Jones:
Burial: White Hill Baptist Church, Lula, Georgia

50.   **Jonathan Amos** was born about 1791 in North Carolina. He died in 1859 in McIntosh County, Georgia. He married **Mary Ann Rozier** in 1830.

51.   **Mary Ann Rozier** was born about 1814 in Wayne County, Georgia. She died on 17 Mar 1897 in McIntosh County, Georgia.

More About Jonathan Amos:
Living In: 1850 McIntosh County, Georgia

More About Mary Ann Rozier:
Burial: Plum Orchard Cemetery, Cox, McIntosh County, Georgia
Living In: 1860 McIntosh County, Georgia

Notes for Mary Ann Rozier:
Headstone spells her maiden name as Rozer.

Mary Ann Rozier and Jonathan Amos had the following children:
i.   James David Amos, son of Jonathan Amos and Mary Ann Rozier was born about 1833 in McIntosh County, Georgia.

ii.   Olive Amos, daughter of Jonathan Amos and Mary Ann Rozier was born about 1834 in McIntosh County, Georgia.

25. iii. Sarah Amos, daughter of Jonathan Amos and Mary Ann Rozier was born about 1835 in Georgia. She died on 16 May 1906 in Georgia. She married Jabez D. Ryals. He was born about 1826 in Georgia. He died on 01 Aug 1904 in Georgia.

iv. William Amos, son of Jonathan Amos and Mary Ann Rozier was born about 1836 in McIntosh County, Georgia.

v. Joseph Amos, son of Jonathan Amos and Mary Ann Rozier was born about 1838 in McIntosh County, Georgia.

vi. Henry Amos, son of Jonathan Amos and Mary Ann Rozier was born about 1840 in McIntosh County, Georgia.

vii. Amanda Amos, daughter of Jonathan Amos and Mary Ann Rozier was born on 01 May 1845 in McIntosh County, Georgia. She died on 21 Oct 1909.

More About Amanda Amos:
Burial: Plum Orchard Cemetery, Cox, McIntosh County, Georgia

viii. Louisa Amos, daughter of Jonathan Amos and Mary Ann Rozier was born on 16 May 1847 in McIntosh County, Georgia.

ix. Mary Ann Amos, daughter of Jonathan Amos and Mary Ann Rozier was born on 03 May 1849 in McIntosh County, Georgia.

56. **Curtis Deal**, son of Simon A. Deal and Sintha Williams was born about 1814 in North Carolina. He died after 1870 in Georgia. He married **Frances Gill** on 05 Jul 1835 in Telfair County, Georgia.

57. **Frances Gill** was born in 1810 in Tellfair County, Georgia. She died in 1851 in Tellfair County, Georgia.

58.

More About Curtis Deal:
Burial: Mount Olivet Cemetery, Liberty County, Georgia
Living In: 1850 Telfair County, Georgia
Living In: 1860 Liberty County, Georgia
Living In: 1870 Living with his son John Deal in McIntosh County, Georgia

Frances Gill and Curtis Deal had the following children:
i. Sarah Deal, daughter of Curtis Deal and Frances Gill was born about 1836 in Georgia.

ii. Zachariah Deal, son of Curtis Deal and Frances Gill was born on 24 Feb 1838 in Telfair County, Georgia. He died on 29 Nov 1919 in Liberty County, Georgia. He married Alice Alethea Jackson, daughter of Joseph Jackson and Mary Ann Somersall on 27 Mar 1862. She was born on 27 Oct 1843 in Liberty County, Georgia. She died on 15 Aug 1915 in Darien, McIntosh County, Georgia.

More About Zachariah Deal:
Burial: Dean's Grove Cemetery, Jones, McIntosh County, Georgia
Military Service: August 27, 1861, Company H, 25Th Georgia Infantry, C.S.A.

Notes for Zachariah Deal:
Company H, 25th Georgia Infantry was known as company E then company G before becoming company H.

More About Alice Alethea Jackson:
Burial: Dean's Grove Cemetery, Jones, McIntosh County, Georgia

    iii.   Jacob J. Deal, son of Curtis Deal and Frances Gill was born about 1841 in Georgia.

    iv.   Cornelius Deal, son of Curtis Deal and Frances Gill was born about 1844 in Georgia.

    v.   Eliza M. Deal, daughter of Curtis Deal and Frances Gill was born about 1845 in Georgia.

    vi.   Drucilla Deal, daughter of Curtis Deal and Frances Gill was born about 1846 in Georgia. She died in 1900.

28.   vii. John Washington Deal, son of Curtis Deal and Frances Gill was born in Apr 1848. He died on 21 Nov 1926 in McIntosh County, Georgia. He married Susan Ann Rowe on 16 Jan 1868 in Liberty County, Georgia. She was born in Aug 1843. She died before 21 Nov 1926.

    viii. William Deal, son of Curtis Deal and Frances Gill was born about 1851 in Georgia.

Generation 7

80.   **Jarrett Turner**, son of Micajah Turner and Nancy (unknown) was born on 06 May 1806 in South Carolina. He died on 03 Jan 1857 in Union County, Georgia. He married **Sarah Collins**, daughter of Thompson Collins and Celia (unknown) on 19 Jul 1830 in Habersham County, Georgia.

81.   **Sarah Collins**, daughter of Thompson Collins and Celia (unknown) was born on 16 Feb 1812 in Buncombe County, North Carolina. She died on 16 Jan 1867.

More About Jarrett Turner:
Living In: 1850 Union County, Georgia

More About Sarah Collins:
Living In: 1860 Union County, Georgia

Sarah Collins and Jarrett Turner had the following children:

    i.   Celia Turner, daughter of Jarrett Turner and Sarah Collins was born on 25 Dec 1831 in Habersham County, Georgia.

    ii.   Nancy Turner, daughter of Jarrett Turner and Sarah Collins was born on 29 Nov 1832 in Union County, Georgia.

    iii.   Francis Marion Turner, son of Jarrett Turner and Sarah Collins was born on 24 Aug 1834 in Union County, Georgia.

    iv.   Elizabeth Turner, daughter of Jarrett Turner and Sarah Collins was born on 17 Jan 1836 in Union County, Georgia.

    v.   Ruth Turner, daughter of Jarrett Turner and Sarah Collins was born on 10 Dec 1837 in Union County, Georgia.

40.   vi. James Jarrett Turner, son of Jarrett Turner and Sarah Collins was born on 25 Jul 1840 in Habersham County, Georgia. He died on 30 Sep 1899 in Hall County, Georgia. He married Mary Elizabeth Dyer, daughter of Micajah Dyer and Harriet Hall on 28 Mar 1858 in Union County, Georgia. She was born in 1842 in Union County, Georgia. She died on 10 Nov 1910.

     vii. Sarah Caroline Turner, daughter of Jarrett Turner and Sarah Collins was born on 17 Jun 1842 in Union County, Georgia.

     viii. Phoebe Turner, daughter of Jarrett Turner and Sarah Collins was born on 16 Oct 1844 in Union County, Georgia.

     ix. Micajah Turner, son of Jarrett Turner and Sarah Collins was born on 03 Aug 1847 in Union County, Georgia.

     x. Olive S. Turner, daughter of Jarrett Turner and Sarah Collins was born on 30 Sep 1849 in Union County, Georgia.

     xi. William Pruitt Turner, son of Jarrett Turner and Sarah Collins was born on 21 Apr 1852 in Union County, Georgia.

     xii. Thompson Turner, son of Jarrett Turner and Sarah Collins was born on 29 Jul 1854 in Union County, Georgia.

82. **Micajah Dyer** was born about 1817 in Georgia. He married **Harriet Hall**.

83. **Harriet Hall** was born about 1823 in Georgia.

More About Micajah Dyer:
Living In: 1860 Union County, Georgia
Living In: 1870 Appling County, Georgia
Occupation: Farmer

Harriet Hall and Micajah Dyer had the following children:

41.   i. Mary Elizabeth Dyer, daughter of Micajah Dyer and Harriet Hall was born in 1842 in Union County, Georgia. She died on 10 Nov 1910. She married James Jarrett Turner, son of Jarrett Turner and Sarah Collins on 28 Mar 1858 in Union County, Georgia. He was born on 25 Jul 1840 in Habersham County, Georgia. He died on 30 Sep 1899 in Hall County, Georgia.

     iii. Rosetta A. Dyer, daughter of Micajah Dyer and Harriet Hall was born about 1845.

     iv. Lucinda C. Dyer, daughter of Micajah Dyer and Harriet Hall was born about 1847.

     v. William Dyer, son of Micajah Dyer and Harriet Hall was born about 1852.

     vi. Milldred Dyer, daughter of Micajah Dyer and Harriet Hall was born about 1856.

     vii. Joseph E. Dyer, son of Micajah Dyer and Harriet Hall was born about 1859.

     viii. Andrew J. Dyer, son of Micajah Dyer and Harriet Hall was born about 1867.

90. **James Crow** was born about 1785 in South Carolina.

James Crow had the following child:

45.   i. Mary Ann Crow, daughter of James Crow was born about 1820 in Georgia. She died in 1911. She married Jacob Canup. He was born about 1815 in North Carolina. He died in 1896.

112.   **Simon A. Deal**, son of John Deal and Mary (unknown) was born in 1779 in North Carolina. He died on 07 Nov 1837 in Emanuel County, Georgia. He married **Sintha Williams** on 10 Mar 1804 in Bulloch County, Georgia.

113.   **Sintha Williams** was born in 1780 in Bulloch County, Georgia.

Sintha Williams and Simon A. Deal had the following children:
        i.   Susan Deal, daughter of Simon A. Deal and Sintha Williams was born about 1812.

        ii.   James Deal, son of Simon A. Deal and Sintha Williams was born about 1812. He died in 1854.

57.   iii. Curtis Deal, son of Simon A. Deal and Sintha Williams was born about 1814 in North Carolina. He died after 1870 in Georgia. He married Frances Gill on 05 Jul 1835 in Telfair County, Georgia. She was born in 1810 in Tellfair County, Georgia. She died in 1851 in Tellfair County, Georgia.

        iv.   William A. Deal, son of Simon A. Deal and Sintha Williams was born about 1816. He died in 1864.

Generation 8

160.   **Micajah Turner** was born in 1777 in Virginia. He died on 01 Nov 1871 in Cleveland, White County, Georgia. He married **Nancy (unknown)** in 1795 in Virginia.

161.   **Nancy (unknown)** was born in 1777 in Virginia. She died about 1875 in White County, Georgia.

More   About   Micajah
Turner:
Burial: Tesnatee Baptist Church Cemetery, Cleveland, White County, Georgia
Living In: 1850 Habersham County, Georgia
Living In: 1860 White County, Georgia
Living In: 1870 White County, Georgia

Notes for Micajah Turner:
Date of death is from headstone at Tesnatee Baptist Church Cemetery.

More About Nancy (unknown):
Burial: Tesnatee Baptist Church Cemetery, Cleveland, White County, Georgia

Nancy (unknown) and Micajah Turner had the following children:
        i.   Joseph Turner, son of Micajah Turner and Nancy (unknown) was born about 1796 in South Carolina.

        ii.   John Berryman Turner, son of Micajah Turner and Nancy (unknown) was born on 01 May 1798 in South Carolina.

        iii. Henry Turner, son of Micajah Turner and Nancy (unknown) was born about 1800 in South Carolina. He married Celia (unknown). She was born about 1806 in North Carolina.

More About Henry Turner:
Living In: 1850 Habersham County, Georgia
Living In: Bet. 1860-1880 White County, Georgia

Notes for Henry Turner:
Living next door to his parents in 1870.

    iv.   Susannah Turner, daughter of Micajah Turner and Nancy (unknown) was born about 1802 in South Carolina.

    v.   William Turner, son of Micajah Turner and Nancy (unknown) was born about 1805 in South Carolina.

80.   vi. Jarrett Turner, son of Micajah Turner and Nancy (unknown) was born on 06 May 1806 in South Carolina. He died on 03 Jan 1857 in Union County, Georgia. He married Sarah Collins, daughter of Thompson Collins and Celia (unknown) on 19 Jul 1830 in Habersham County, Georgia. She was born on 16 Feb 1812 in Buncombe County, North Carolina. She died on 16 Jan 1867.

    vii.   Jesse Turner, son of Micajah Turner and Nancy (unknown) was born about 1808 in South Carolina.

    viii.   Sabray Turner, daughter of Micajah Turner and Nancy (unknown) was born about 1810 in South Carolina.

    ix.   Hiram Turner, son of Micajah Turner and Nancy (unknown) was born about 1811 in South Carolina.

    x.   Butler Turner, son of Micajah Turner and Nancy (unknown) was born between 1815-1820 in Habersham County, Georgia.

    xi.   Nancy Turner, daughter of Micajah Turner and Nancy (unknown) was born on 16 Jul 1825 in Habersham County, Georgia.

    xii.   Micajah Turner, son of Micajah Turner and Nancy (unknown) was born in 1830 in Habersham County, Georgia.

162.   **Thompson Collins** was born about 1785 in Buncombe County, North Carolina. He died about 1858 in Union County, Georgia. He married **Celia (unknown)** in 1810 in Buncombe County, North Carolina.

163.   **Celia (unknown)** was born about 1787 in Ashville, North carolina.

Celia (unknown) and Thompson Collins had the following children:

    i.   Archibald Cale Collins, son of Thompson Collins and Celia (unknown) was born in 1811 in Buncombe County, North Carolina.

    ii.   Elizabeth Collins, daughter of Thompson Collins and Celia (unknown) was born on 12 Aug 1814 in Buncombe County, North Carolina.

82.   iii. Sarah Collins, daughter of Thompson Collins and Celia (unknown) was born on 16 Feb 1812 in Buncombe County, North Carolina. She died on 16 Jan 1867. She married Jarrett Turner, son of Micajah Turner and Nancy (unknown) on 19 Jul 1830 in Habersham County, Georgia. He was born on 06 May 1806 in South Carolina. He died on 03 Jan 1857 in Union County, Georgia.

iv. Francis Collins, son of Thompson Collins and Celia (unknown) was born on 28 Dec 1816 in Buncombe County, North Carolina.

v. Thompson Collins, son of Thompson Collins and Celia (unknown) was born in Nov 1818 in Buncombe County, North Carolina.

vi. Ruth Collins, daughter of Thompson Collins and Celia (unknown) was born in 1820 in Buncombe County, North Carolina.

vii. Celia Collins, daughter of Thompson Collins and Celia (unknown) was born in 1826 in Habersham County, Georgia.

viii. Nancy Collins, daughter of Thompson Collins and Celia (unknown) was born on 13 Feb 1829 in Habersham County, Georgia.

ix. Olive Collins, daughter of Thompson Collins and Celia (unknown) was born on 12 May 1831 in Habersham County, Georgia.

x. Ivan Kimsey Collins, son of Thompson Collins and Celia (unknown) was born on 19 Apr 1835 in Union County, Georgia.

224. **John Deal** was born in 1761 in North Carolina. He died in 1818 in Emanuel County, Georgia. He married **Mary (unknown)** in 1778.

225. **Mary (unknown)** was born in 1754. She died in 1823.

Mary (unknown) and John Deal had the following child:

112. i. Simon A. Deal, son of John Deal and Mary (unknown) was born in 1779 in North Carolina. He died on 07 Nov 1837 in Emanuel County, Georgia. He married Sintha Williams on 10 Mar 1804 in Bulloch County, Georgia. She was born in 1780 in Bulloch County, Georgia.

Descendants of Mark Edward Simmons

Generation 1

1. **MARK EDWARD**[1] **SIMMONS** was born on 29 Oct 1967. He married (1) **DIANA GAIL EDWARDS** on 23 Dec 1988 in Plant City, Florida. She was born on 28 Mar 1969 in Plant City, Florida. He married **SHERRI (UNKNOWN)**. He married **NANCY SANTIAGO CLARIDY**.

Mark Edward Simmons and Diana Gail Edwards had the following children:

    i. MARK GREGORY[2] EDWARDS was born on 20 Jun 1988 in Plant City, Florida. He married Julie Ann Mercer on 17 Feb 2007 in Wellston, Ohio. She was born on 28 May 1988.

    ii. DAVIAN GAIL SIMMONS was born on 12 Feb 1991 in Monroe, North Carolina. She married Jerrod Elden Rogers, son of James J. Rogers and Betty Lou Eberts on 24 Mar 2012 in Berlin Crossroads, Jackson County, Ohio. He was born on 17 Mar 1987 in Ohio.

Mark Edward Simmons and Sherri (unknown) had the following child:

4.   iii. MARISSA DAWN (UNKNOWN) was born on 11 Aug 1987. She married JARED REEVES. He was born on 28 Feb 1988.

Mark Edward Simmons and Nancy Santiago Claridy had the following child:

5.   iv. ASHLEY NICOLE SIMMONS was born on 21 Oct 1985. She married JUSTIN HELMS. He was born on 26 Jan 1986.

Generation 2

2   **MARK GREGORY**[2] **EDWARDS** (Mark Gregory[1] Simmons) was born on 20 Jun 1988 in Plant City, Florida. He married Julie Ann Mercer on 17 Feb 2007 in Wellston, Ohio. She was born on 28 May 1988.

Mark Gregory Edwards and Julie Ann Mercer had the following children:

    1.   SOPHIA MARIE[3] EDWARDS was born on 05 Aug 2010 in Chillicothe, Ohio.

    2.   MARK WILTON EDWARDS was born on 28 Oct 2013 in Columbus, Ohio.

3   **DAVIAN GAIL**[2] **SIMMONS** (Mark Edward[1]) was born on 12 Feb 1991 in Monroe, North Carolina. She married Jerrod Elden Rogers, son of James J. Rogers and Betty Lou Eberts on 24 Mar 2012 in Berlin Crossroads, Jackson County, Ohio. He was born on 17 Mar 1987 in Ohio.

Jerrod Elden Rogers and Davian Gail Simmons had the following children:

    1.   DAVID[3] ROGERS was born on 03 May 2014 in Athens, Ohio.

    2.   CLOE GAIL ROGERS was born on 14 May 2016 in Athens, Ohio.

4   **MARISSA DAWN**[2] **(UNKNOWN)** (Mark Edward[1] Simmons) was born on 11 Aug 1987. She married **JARED REEVES**. He was born on 28 Feb 1988.

Jared Reeves and Marissa Dawn (unknown) had the following child:

    1.   COLTON[3] REEVES was born on 18 Oct 2013.

5   **ASHLEY NICOLE**[2] **SIMMONS** (Mark Edward[1]) was born on 21 Oct 1985. She married **JUSTIN HELMS**. He was born on 26 Jan 1986.

Justin Helms and Ashley Nicole Simmons had the following children:

    1.   AUDRA DENISE[3] HELMS was born on 02 Nov 2009.

Generation 2 (con't)

2. JUSTIN LEVI HELMS was born on 15 Mar 2015.